The Lives Of The Most Eminent English Poets

Samuel Johnson

Nabu Public Domain Reprints:

You are holding a reproduction of an original work published before 1923 that is in the public domain in the United States of America, and possibly other countries. You may freely copy and distribute this work as no entity (individual or corporate) has a copyright on the body of the work. This book may contain prior copyright references, and library stamps (as most of these works were scanned from library copies). These have been scanned and retained as part of the historical artifact.

This book may have occasional imperfections such as missing or blurred pages, poor pictures, errant marks, etc. that were either part of the original artifact, or were introduced by the scanning process. We believe this work is culturally important, and despite the imperfections, have elected to bring it back into print as part of our continuing commitment to the preservation of printed works worldwide. We appreciate your understanding of the imperfections in the preservation process, and hope you enjoy this valuable book.

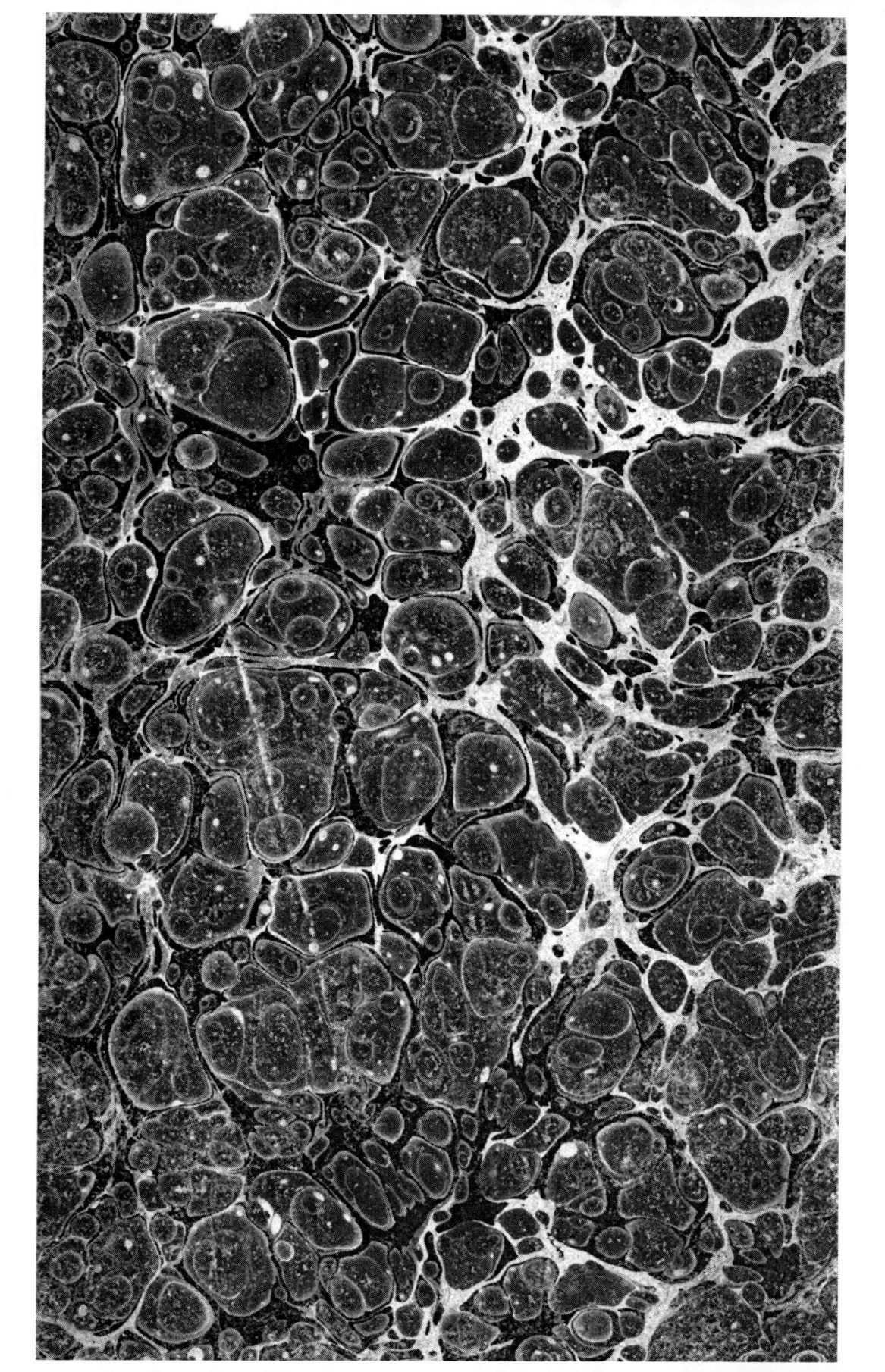

Ex Libris
R. W. Chapman

Parker
Aug 15 '44

Additions and
Lives of the Po[ets]
1781 is a mere r[eprint?]
than Johnson r[ead?]
the booksellers
who had the [ ]
applications. [ ]
sheets, having [ ]
them from h[im?]

Letters and Journals of
F.S. of the Harte Park (1779-81),
his expedition to the Villages

Parker
Aug 15 94

THE PRINCIPAL

ADDITIONS and CORRECTIONS

IN THE THIRD EDITION OF

Dr. JOHNSON's

LIVES OF THE POETS;

COLLECTED TO COMPLETE

THE SECOND EDITION.

THE PRINCIPAL

ADDITIONAL CORRECTIONS

TO THE THIRD EDITION OF

Dr. JOHNSON'S

LIVES OF THE POETS,

COLLECTED COMPLETE

THE FOURTH EDITION.

ADDITIONS and CORRECTIONS.

VOLUME I.

Page v. line 12. read Mr. Steevens and other friends.

COWLEY.

P. 5. l. 4. r. Sir Joshua Reynolds, the great Painter of the present age.

P. 10. l. 9. *add*, V. Barnesii Anacreontem.

P. 27. l. 15. *dele* the last of the race.

P. 58. l. 15 and 16. r. not so much to move the affections, as to exercise the understanding.

P. 60. l. 22. r. to rate his own, &c.

P. 77. l. 13. *add*, and by Dryden, in Mac Flecnoe, it has once been imitated.

Ib. l. 17. r. Of this silence and neglect.

P. 82. l. 13. *add*, he offends by exaggeration as much as by diminution.

P. 91. l. 14. *add*, Jonson and Donne, as Dr. Hurd remarks, were then in the highest esteem.

P. 97. l. 9. r. Yet, amidst his negligence, he sometimes attempted, &c.

P. 98. l. 20. r. columt.

DENHAM.

P. 119. l. 13. r. of a judgment naturally right.

MILTON.

P. 126. l. 22. r. so honourably by chamber-practice, that soon, &c.

P. 130.

ADDITIONS IN VOL. I.

P. 130. l. 12. *add*,

    Me tenet urbs reflua quam Thamesis alluit undâ,
        Meque nec invitum patria dulcis habet.
    Jam nec, &c. — — — — meo.
    Si fit hoc *exilium* patrios adiiffe penates,
        Et vacuum curis otia grata fequi,
    Non ego vel *profugi* nomen fortemve recufo,
        Lætus et *exilii* conditione fruor.

P. 131. l. 4. *add*, And it may be conjectured from the willingnefs with which he has perpetuated the memory of his exile, that its caufe was fuch as gave him no fhame.

P. 143. l. 25. *r*. Phyfiological learning.

P. 160. l. 25. *after* fays, *add*, as Ker, and I think fome one before him, has remarked.

P. 162. l. 3. *add*, from which, however, he was difmiffed, not with any mark of contempt, but with a train of attendance fcarce lefs than regal.

P. 163. l. 23. *r*. office of Latin fecretary.

P. 167. l. 1. *r*. fubfifts only in your abilities.

P. 168. l. ult. *r*. to have refumed three great works which he had planned.

P. 169. l. 14. *r*. ufe of thefe collections.

P. 170. l. 8. *r*. as he hints in his verfes, &c.

P. 178. l. 19. *r*. now about to be reftored.

P. 199. l. 9. *add*, In the hiftory of *Paradife Loft*, a deduction thus minute will rather gratify than fatigue.

P. 200. l. 9. *r*. The call for books.

Ib. l. 16. *r*. a clofet of knowledge.

P. 211. *r*. fed without excefs in quantity, and in his earlier years without delicacy of choice.

P. 255. l. 7. *add*, None ever wifhed it longer than it is.

P. 268. *r*. therefore we reverence that vigour, &c.

BUT-

ADDITIONS IN VOL. I.

BUTLER.

P. 271. l. 10—15. r. Samuel Butler was born in the parish of Stbensham, in Worcestershire; according to his biographer, in 1612. This account Dr. Nash finds confirmed by the register: he was christened Feb. 14.

P. 272. l. 3. r. but Mr. Longueville, the son of Butler's principal friend, says, &c.

Ib. l. 20. *add*, Dr. Nash has discovered that his father was owner of a house and a little land, worth about eight pounds a year, still called *Butler's Tenement*.

P. 273. l. 13. *add*, Some pictures said to be his were shewn to Dr. Nash at Earl's Cromb; but when he enquired for them some years afterwards, he found them destroyed, to stop windows; and owns, that they hardly deserved a better fate.

P. 278. l. 13. *add*, and perhaps his health might now begin to fail.

Ib l. 19. *add*, Granger was informed by Dr. Pearce, who named for his authority Mr. Lowndes of the Treasury, that Butler had an yearly pension of an hundred pounds. This is contradicted by all tradition, by the complaints of Oldham, and by the reproaches of Dryden; and I am afraid will never be confirmed.

P. 280. l. 8. *dele* the date of his birth is doubtful.

P. 281. l. 10. r. to trains of, &c.

P. 290. l. 25. r. which perplexed doctrine, disordered practice, and disturbed, &c.

ROCHESTER.

P. 303. l. 17. r. thirty-fourth year.

P. 307. l. 21. r. of Rochester, whose *buffoon conceit* was, I suppose, a saying often mentioned, that *every man would be a coward if he durst*.

ROSCOMMON.

P. 315. l. a. r. was the son of James Dillon and Elizabeth Wentworth, sister to the earl of Strafford. He was born in Ireland, during the lieutenancy of Strafford, who, being both his uncle and godfather, gave him his own surname. His father, the third earl of Roscommon, had been, &c.

P. 316. l. 9. r. was sent to Caen.

OTWAY.

P. 341. l. 17. r. where he is said to have died of want.

P. 342. l. 1. All this, I hope, is not true; and there is this ground of better hope, that Pope, who lived near enough to be well informed, relates in Spence's Memorials, that he died of a fever caught by violent pursuit of a thief that had robbed one of his friends; but that indigence, and its concomitants, sorrow and despondency, pressed hard upon him, has never been denied, whatever immediate cause might bring him to the grave.

WALLER.

P. 349. l. 5. r. Neither of these pieces, that seem to carry their own dates, could have been the sudden effusion of fancy. In the verses on the prince's escape, the prediction of his marriage, &c.

Ib. l. 11. r. could not be properly perused.

P. 353. l. 10. r. praised some whom, &c.

P. 364. l. ult. r. They proceeded with great caution. Three only met in one place, and no man was allowed to impart the plot to more than two others; so that if any should be suspected or seized, more than three could not be endangered.

P. 365. l. 13. r. for the Royalists.

ADDITIONS IN VOL. I.

P. 365. l. 15. r. there were five for them.

P. 368. l. 12. r. May, 1643.

P. 375. l. 13. *add*, His crime was, that he had commission to raise money for the King; but it appears not that the money was to be expended upon the advancement of either Crisp or Waller's plot.

Ib. l. 23. r. Hampden escaped death, perhaps by the interest of his family; but, &c.

P. 395. l. 14. r. he endeavored the improvement.

P. 420. l. 7. *add*, and in another play, the Sonnet of Holofernes fully displays it.

POMFRET

P. 432. l. ult. r. some species of merit.

DORSET

P. 435. l. 5. r. as the author is so generally read.

STEPNEY

P. 443. l. 6. r. where he passed six years in the college, he went at nineteen to Cambridge.

P. 445. l. 3. r. superaverit.

Ib. l. 6. r. parum, Famæ &c.

Ib. l. 7. r. essayit.

PHILIPS

P. 454. l. 4. r. non quod

P. 459. l. 3. r. generally alluring.

WALSH

P. 477. l. penult. r. a scholar, but a man of fashion; and, ad Dennis's remarks, ostentatiously splendid in his dress.

VOLUME II.

DRYDEN.

P. 4. l. 16. *After* patrimony, *r.* He was indeed sometimes reproached for his first religion. I am therefore inclined to believe that Derrick's intelligence was partly true, and partly erroneous.

P. 8. l. 2. *r.* but since the plays are said to be printed, &c.

P. 11. l. 10. *r.* which may be esteemed one, &c.

P. 49. l. 18. *add.* When this was first brought upon the stage, news that the Duke of Monmouth had landed was told in the theatre, upon which the company departed, and Arthur was exhibited no more.

P. 51. l. 21. *r.* copiously as occasions arose.

P. 59. l. 30. *r.* Fanshaw, Denham, &c.

P. 83. l. ult. *r.* nor have I met with any confirmation but in a letter of Farquhar, and he only relates that the funeral of Dryden was tumultuous and confused. Supposing the thing true, we may remark that the gradual change of manners, &c.

P. 100. l. 6. *r.* helpless misery.

P. 106. l. 1. *r.* One of his opinions will, &c.

Ib. l. 5. *r.* He put great confidence

Ib. l. 11. *dele* and, &c. *to* true, l. 13.

P. 107. l. 2. *add,* The letter added to this narrative leaves no room to doubt of his notions or practice.

P. 108. l. 16. *r.* regular and valuable treatise.

P. 112. l. 18. *r.* poured out his knowledge with a little labour.

P. 123. l. 6. *r.* should transmit to things.

P. 130. l. 4. *r.* Davenant was perhaps at this time

P. 134. l. 12. *r.* gives the reader

P. 137.

ADDITIONS IN VOL. III.

P. 137. l. 8. *add*, for he complains of its difficulty.
P. 155. l. 22. *r.* what durable materials.
P. 179. l. 7. *r.* by reviving natural sentiments, or impressing new appearances of things.
Ib. l. 18. *r.* are not always understood.
Ib. l. 24. *r.* objections and solutions at command.
P. 193. l. 3, 4. Though Davis has reasoned in rhyme before him, it may be perhaps maintained that he was the first who joined argument with poetry.

SMITH.

P. 247. l. 3, 4. *r.* the censor is a tutor, and it was not thought proper, &c.
P. 260. l. 17. *r.* versuum ordinem &c.
P. 261. l. 11. *Flacco*] Pro *Flacco*, animo paulo attentiore, scripsissem *Marone*.

DUKE.

P. 266. l. 14. *r.* been bad in the first part of his life was, &c.

KING.

P. 273. l. 14. *add*, on a question which Learning only could decide.
Ib. l. 16. *after* Lister, *add*, who had published *A Journey to Paris*.

SPRAT.

P. 289. l. 7. *r.* by my father, an old man.

HALIFAX.

P. 299. l. 21. *r.* and, if the patron be an author, those &c.

PARNELL.

P. 304. l. 4. *r.* to the memory of Goldsmith.

ADDITIONS IN VOL. II.

GARTH.

P. 319. l. 21. *add*, Pope afterwards declared himself convinced that Garth died in the communion of the Church of Rome, having been privately reconciled. It is observed by Lowth, that there is less distance than is thought between scepticism and popery, and that a mind wearied with perpetual doubt, willingly seeks repose in the bosom of an infallible church.

ROWE.

P. 325. l. 8. *r.* wholly to elegant literature.

ADDISON.

P. 351. l. 16. *r.* friendship was afterwards too weak.

Ib. l. 19. *r.* Such at least is, &c.

P. 353. l. 1. *r.* In 1697 appeared his Latin verses on &c.

P. 354. l. 7. *add*, because his pension was not remitted.

P. 362. l. 16. *r.* to shew when to speak.

Ib. l. 18. *r.* we had many books.

P. 365. l. 1. *r.* adjusted, like Casa, &c. by propriety &c.

Ib. l. 16. *r.* are now partly known.

P. 377. l. 23. *r.* Steele did not know by any direct testimony.

P. 378. l. ult. *add*, laid hold on no attention, has naturally &c.

P. 379. l. 3. *r.* in which is employed.

Ib. l. 15. *r.* superiority of his powers.

P. 401. l. 4. *add*, One slight lineament of his character Swift has preserved. It was his practice, when he found any man invincibly wrong, to flatter his opinions by acquiescence, and sink him yet deeper in absurdity. This artifice of mischief was admired by Stella, and Swift seems to approve her admiration.

P. 409. l. 13. *r.* In the poem now examined.

P. 441.

P. 441. l. 3. r. the criticism would perhaps have been admired, and the poem still &c.

Ib. l. 24. r. by obscuring its appearances and weakening its effects.

P. 444. l. 7. r. It was apparently his &c.

HUGHES.

P. 455. l. 1. r. too grave a poet for me.

Ib. ult. *add*, In Spence's collections Pope is made to speak of him with still less respect, as having no claim to poetical reputation but from his tragedy.

SHEFFIELD.

P. 459. l. 15. r. as those years, &c. were spent by him, &c.

P. 469. l. 14. r. after the first appearance of the Essay.

VOLUME III.

PRIOR.

P. 7. l. 12. r. was too diligent to miss.

P. 9. l. 4. r. and none ever denied, &c.

P. 13. l. 1. r. brought with him the abbé Gualtier, and M. Mesnager, a minister from France, invested with full powers.

P. 22. l. ult. r. in Hiberniâ.

CONGREVE.

P. 50. l. 24. r. of very powerful and fertile faculties.

BLACKMORE.

P. 73. l. 17. r. at the university; and which he seems to have passed with very little attention to the business of the place; for in his poems the ancient names of nations or places, which he often introduces, are pronounced by chance.

P. 94. l. 5. r. He had likewise written.

P. 102. l. 6. *add*, his works may be read a long time without the occurrence of a single line that stands prominent from the rest.

FENTON.

P. 118. l. ult. *add*, Whatever I have said of Fenton is confirmed by Pope in a Letter, by which he communicated to Brome an account of his death.

TO

The Rev^d. Mr. BROOME

At PULHAM, near HARLESTONE

NOR
SUFFOLKE

By BECCLES Bag.

D^r SIR.

I intended to write to you on this melancholy subject, the death of Mr. Fenton, before y^r came; but stay'd to have inform'd myself and you of ye circumstances of it. All I hear is, that he felt a Gradual Decay, tho so early in Life, and was declining for 5 or 6 months. It was not, as I apprehended, the Gout in his Stomach, but I believe rather a Complication first of Gross Humours, as he was naturally corpulent, not discharging themselves, as he used no sort of Exercise. No man better bore ye approaches of his Dissolution (as I am told) or with less ostentation yielded up his Being. The great Modesty wch you know was natural to him, and ye great contempt he had for all sorts of Vanity and Parade, never appeared more than in his last moments: He had a conscious Satisfaction

(no

(no doubt) in acting right, in feeling himself honest, true, & un-pretending to more than his own. So he dyed, as he lived, with that secret, yet sufficient, Contentment.

As to any Papers left behind him, I dare say they can be but few; for this reason, He never wrote out of Vanity, or thought much of the applause of Men. I know an instance where he did his utmost to Conceal his own merit that way; and if we join to this his natural Love of Ease, I fancy we must expect little of this sort: at least I hear of none except some few remarks on Waller (wch his cautious integrity made him leave an order to be given to Mr. Tonson) and perhaps, tho tis many years since I saw it, a Translation of ye first Book of Oppian. He had begun a Tragedy of Dion, but made small progress in it.

As to his other Affairs, he died poor, but honest, leaving no Debts, or Legacies; except of a few p^{ds} to Mr. Trumbull and my Lady, in token of respect, Gratefulness, & mutual Esteem.

I shall with pleasure take upon me to draw this amiable, quiet, deserving, unpretending, Christian and Philosophical character, in His Epitaph. There Truth may be spoken in a few words: as for Flourish, & Oratory, & Poetry, I leave them to younger and more lively Writers, such as love writing for writing sake, & w^d rather show their own Fine Parts, y^n Report the valuable ones of any other man. So the Elegy I renounce.

I condole with you from my heart, on the loss of so worthy a man, and a Friend to us both. Now he is gone, I must tell you he has done you many a good office, & set your character in ye fairest light, to some who either mistook you, or knew you not. I doubt not he has done the same for me.

Adieu;

Adieu: Let us love his Memory, and profit by his example. I am very sincerely

DR SIR

Your affectionate

& real Servant

A. POPE.

Aug 29th 1730.

GAY.

P. 126. l. 16. r. may naturally imply.

P. 137. l. 13. r. Allegorical Profopopœias,

Ib. l. 23. r. an abstracted Allegory,

P. 138. ult. *add*, The story of the Apparition is borrowed from one of the Tales of Poggio.

YALDEN.

P. 166. l. r. splendid set.

P. 168. l. 10. r. though the rhymes.

TICKELL.

P. 175. l. 6. r. "There had been a coldness," said Mr. Pope.

SOMERVILE.

P. 191. l. 6. r. his house, where he was born in 1692, is called Edston, a seat inherited from a long line of ancestors, for he was said to be of the first family in his county. He tells of himself, that he was born near the Avon's banks. He was bred at Winchester-school, and was elected fellow of New-college. It does not appear that in the places of his education he exhibited any uncommon proofs of genius or literature. His powers were first displayed in the country, where he was

was distinguished as a poet, a gentleman, and a skilful Justice of the Peace.

P. 192. l. 18. r. He died July 19, 1742, and was buried at Wotten, near Henly in Arden. His distresses need not be much pitied; his estate is said to be fifteen hundred a year, which by his death has devolved to lord Somervile of Scotland. His mother indeed, who lived till ninety, had a jointure of six hundred.

P. 193. l. 17 r. are commonly such &c.

SAVAGE.

P. 369. l. 5. *add*, Henley, in one of his advertisements, had mentioned *Pope's Treatment of Savage*. This was supposed by Pope to be the consequence of a complaint made by Savage to Henley, and was therefore mentioned by him with much resentment.

Ib. l. 18. r. July 31, 1743.

P. 371. l. 19. r. as others in their closets.

P. 376. l. 14. r. any foregoing work.

P. 378. l. 4. r. the down of plenty.

SWIFT.

P. 395. l. 5. 17. r. an explanation of an *Ancient Prophecy*, part written after the facts, and the rest never completed, but well planned to excite amazement.

P. 398. l. 20. r. was not made of the ardour, &c.

P. 404. l. 20. r. to have preserved the kindness of the great when they wanted him no longer.

P. 406. l. 16. r. the wish for a life of ease was always returning.

P. 409. l. 9. r. received with respect.

P. 414. l. 19. r. The effect of the publication upon the Dean and Stella.

ADDITIONS IN VOL. III.

P. 423. l. 8. r. a languishing decay.
Ib. l. 11. r. his papers shew.
Ib. l. 21. r. different from the general course.
P. 424. l. 21. r. died under the tyranny.
P. 425. l. 11. r. Swift himself has, &c.
P. 436. l. 8. r. it is the best mode, but &c.
P. 437. l. 4. r. To his duty as Dean he was very attentive.
P. 444. l. 3. r. an assumed imperiousness.

VOLUME IV.

POPE.

P. 4. l. 6. r. was never discovered till Mr. Tyers told, on the authority of Mrs. Racket, that he was a linen-draper in the Strand.

P. 37. l. 21. r. Lintot printed two hundred and fifty on royal paper in folio for two guineas a volume; of the small folio, having printed seventeen hundred and fifty copies of the first volume, he reduced the number in the other volumes to a thousand.

P. 38. l. 18. Of this edition two thousand five hundred were first printed, and five thousand a few weeks afterwards.

P. 41. l. 15. r. could easily obtain.

P. 43. l. 17. *add*, and who professed to have forgotten the terms on which he worked.

P. 45. l. 17. *add*, and only six hundred and sixty were printed.

P. 67. l. 14. r. were not long divided.

P. 105. l. 7. r. together with a fancy &c.

P. 105.

ADDITIONS IN VOL. IV.

P. 105. l. 18. *r.* and excited against the advocate the wishes of some who favoured the cause.

P. 106. l. 9. *r.* He tells Concanen, " *Dryden* I observe borrows for want of leasure, and *Pope* for want of genius; *Milton* out of pride, and *Addison* out of modesty."

P. 126. l. 3. *r.* unattainable Arts.

P. 132. l. 6. *r.* his father the painter.

P. 133. l. 16. *r.* with terminations not consistent with the time or country in which he places them.

P. 137. l. 9. *r.* He left the care of his papers to his executors, first to lord Bolingbroke, and if he should not be living to the earl of Marchmont, undoubtedly expecting them to be proud of the trust.

Ib. l. 14. *r.* Dodsley the bookseller went to solicit, &c.

P. 140. l. 17. *add,* To this apology an answer was written, in *A Letter to the most impudent man living.*

P. 142. l. 4. *r.* and by another is described, &c.

P. 151. l. 19. *r.* The name of Congreve appears in the Letters among those of his other friends, but without any observable distinction or consequence.

P. 153. l. 22. *r.* which men give of their own minds.

P. 170. l. 13. *r.* Almost every line.

Ib. l. 17. *r.* almost every line.

P. 177. l. 12. *r.* it never obtained.

P. 184. l. 3. *r.* without much attention.

P. 195. l. 21. *r.* will be found, in the progress of learning.

P. 200. l. 10. *r.* was to him a new study; he was &c.

Ib. l. 18. *r.* He finds out that those Beings must be *somewhere,* and that *all,* &c.

P. 206. l. 17. *r.* and by which extrinsick, &c.

ADDITIONS IN VOL. IV.

P. 209. l. 6. *add*, In his latter productions the diction is sometimes vitiated by French idioms, with which Bolingbroke had perhaps infected him.

P. 224. l. 16. *r.* where is the relation between the two positions, that he *gained no title,* and *lost no friend?*

P. 230. l. 12. *r,* is borrowed from Dryden.

P. 231. l. 5. *r.* is borrowed from the epitaph on Raphael.

P. 233. l. 14. *r.* is borrowed from Crashaw.

P. 234. l. 20. *r.* is not more successfully executed than the rest, for it will not &c.

P. 239. l. 20. *r.* even this wretchedness,

P. 240. l. 11. *r.* haberet is sepulchrum.

Ib. l. 12. *r.* Surely Ariosto did not venture to expect that his trifle would have ever had such an illustrious imitator.

PITT.

P. 244. l. 18. *r.* Tristram's splendid edition.

P. 246. l. 6. *add*, This can hardly be true; and, if true, is nothing to the reader.

Ib. l. 10. *r.* He gave us a complete English Eneid, which I am sorry not to see joined in the late publication with his other poems.

THOMSON.

P. 263. l. 6. *add*, and was welcomed to the theatre by a general clap; he had much regard for Thomson, and once expressed it in a Poetical Epistle sent to Italy, of which, however, he abated the value, by transplanting some of the lines into his Epistle to *Arbuthnot.*

P. 264. l. 6. It may be doubted whether he was, either &c.

P. 274. l. ult. *add*, The highest praise which he has received ought not to be suppressed; it is said by lord Lyttelton in the prologue to his posthumous play, that his works contained

"No line which, dying, he could wish to blot."

WATT

WATTS.

P. 286. l. 16. ult. *after* annual revenue, *add*, though the whole was not a hundred a year.

P. 287. l. 20. *r.* to admire his meekness of opposition, and his mildness of censure.

P. 291. l. 3. *r.* his fancy was to be supplied.

A. PHILIPS.

P. 300. l. 16. *r.* variety of matter, which &c.

P. 301. l. 16, 17. *r.* to censure.

Ib. l. 23. *r. Boschareccie.*

P. 304. l. 17. *r.* the subscriptions for Homer.

WEST.

P. 315. l. 6. *after* 1748, *add*, and would doubtless have reached yet further had he lived to complete what he had for some time meditated, the Evidences of the truth of the New Testament. Perhaps it may not be without effect to tell, that he read the prayers of the Publick Liturgy every morning to his family; and that on Sunday evening he called his servants into the parlour, and read to them, first a sermon, and then prayers.

Ib. l. 20. *add*, These two illustrious friends had for a while listened to the blandishments of infidelity; and when West's book was published, it was bought by some, who did know his change of opinion, in expectation of new objections against Christianity; and as Infidels do not want malignity, they revenged the disappointment by calling him a Methodist.

P. 316. l. 14. *r.* the grave might be without its terrors.

P. 318. l. 13. *r.* has two amusements together.

DYER.

ADDITIONS IN VOL. IV.
DYER.

P. 336. l. 17. r. his acquisitions in painting.

P. 337. l. 9. r. In 1751, Sir John Heathcote gave him Coningsby, of one hundred and forty pounds a year; and in 1755 the Chancellor added Kirkby.

Ib. l. 16. r. In 1757 he published the *Fleece*.

SHENSTONE.

P. 345. l. 3. r. his name in the book ten years.

P. 346. l. 10. r. Now was excited his delight &c.

YOUNG.

P. 370. l. 8. *add*, In Swift's " Rhapsody on Poetry" are these lines, speaking of the court—

 Whence Gay was banish'd in disgrace,
 Where Pope will never show his face,
 Where Y—— must torture his invention
 To flatter knaves, or lose his pension.

That Y—— means Young is clear from four other lines in the same poem.

 Attend, ye Popes and Youngs and Gays,
 And tune your harps and strew your bays;
 Your panegyrics here provide;
 You cannot err on flattery's side.

P. 379. l. 11. r. Of his adventures in the Exeter family I am unable to give any account. His attempt &c.

P. 380. l. 8. *add*, From your account of Tickell it appears that he and Young used to " communicate to each " other whatever verses they wrote, even to the least " things."

P. 382. l. 12. *add*, Her majesty had stood godmother and given her name to a daughter of the lady whom Young marred in 1731.

P. 387. l. 19. *add*, It stood originally so high in the author's opinion, that he intitled the Poem, " Ocean, an Ode.
" Con-

"*Concluding with a Wish.*" This wish consists of thirteen stanzas. The first runs thus:

> O may I *steal*
> Along the *vale*
> Of humble life, secure from foes!
> My friend sincere,
> My judgment clear,
> And gentle business my repose!

The three last stanzas are not more remarkable for just rhymes; but, altogether, they will make rather a curious page in the life of Young.

> Prophetic schemes,
> And golden dreams,
> May I, unsanguine, cast away!
> Have what I *have*,
> And live, not *leave*,
> Enamoured of the present day!
>
> My hours my own!
> My faults unknown!
> My chief revenue in content!
> Then leave one *beam*
> Of honest *fame!*
> And scorn the laboured monument!
>
> Unhurt my urn
> Till that great *turn*
> When mighty nature's self shall die,
> Time cease to glide,
> With human pride,
> Sunk in the ocean of eternity!

P. 388. l. 9. *add*, The next paragraph in his *essay* did not occur to him when he talked of *that great turn* in the stanza just quoted. " But then the writer must take
" care

" care that the difficulty is overcome. That is, he
" must make rhyme confiftent with as perfect fenfe
" and expreffion, as could be expected if he was per-
" fectly free from that fhackle."

Another part of this *Effay* will convict the following ftanza of, what every reader will difcover in it, " involun-
" tary burlefque."

>The northern blaſt,
>The fhattered maſt,
>The ſyrt, the whirlpool, and the rock,
>The breaking ſpout,
>The *ſtars gone out,*
>The boiling ſtreight, the monſter's fhock.

But would the Englifh poets fill quite fo many volumes, if all their productions were to be tried, like this, by an elaborate effay on each particular fpecies of poetry of which they exhibit fpecimens?

If Young be not a Lyric poet, he is at leaft a critic in that fort of poetry; and if his Lyric poetry can be proved bad, it was firſt proved fo by his own criticifm. This furely is candid.

Milbourne was ftyled by Pope *the faireſt of Criticks*, only becaufe he exhibited his own verfion of Virgil to be compared with Dryden's which he condemned, and with which every reader had it otherwife in his power to compare it. Young was furely not the moft unfair of poets for prefixing to a Lyric compofition an effay on Lyric poetry fo juft and impartial as to condemn himfelf.

We fhall foon come to a work, before which we find indeed no critical Effay, but which difdains to fhrink from the touchftone of the fevereft critic; and which certainly,

tainly, as I remember to have heard you say, if it contains some of the worst, contains also some of the best things in the language.

Soon after the appearance of " Ocean," when he was almost fifty, Young entered into Orders.

P. 391. l. 13. *add,* Poetry had lately been taught by Addison to aspire to the arms of nobility, though not with extraordinary happiness.

P. 392. l. ult. *add,* Thomson, in his Autumn, addressing Mr. Dodington, calls his seat the seat of the Muses,

Where, in the secret bower and winding walk,
For virtuous Young and thee they twine the bay.

The praises Thomson bestows but a few lines before on Philips, the second

Who nobly durst, in rhyme-unfettered verse,
With British freedom sing the British song;

added to Thomson's example and success, might perhaps induce Young, as we shall see presently, to write his great work without rhyme.

In 1734, he published *The foreign Address, or the best Argument for Peace; occasioned by the British Fleet and the Posture of Affairs. Written in the Character of a Sailor.* It is not to be found in the author's four volumes.

P. 395. l. 15. *add,* to whom the Prince of Wales was godfather.

P. 396. l. 19. *add,* What he calls " The *true* estimate of " Human Life," which has already been mentioned, exhibits only the wrong side of the tapestry; and being asked why he did not show the right, he is said to have replied he could not—though by others it has been told me that this was finished, but that a Lady's monkey tore it in pieces before there existed any copy.

P. 396.

P. 396. l. ult. *add*, From them who anfwer in the affirmative it fhould not be concealed that, though *Invifibilia non decipiunt* was infcribed upon a deception in Young's grounds, and *ambulantes in horto audiérunt vocem Dei* on a building in his garden; his parifh was indebted to the good-humour of the Author of the Night Thoughts for an affembly and a bowling-green.

P. 403. l. 19. *add*, He who is connected with the Author of the Night Thoughts only by veneration for the Poet and the Chriftian, may be allowed to obferve that Young is one of thofe concerning whom, as you remark in your account of Addifon, it is proper rather to fay " nothing that is falfe than all that is true."

P. 409. l. 7. *add*, Deduct from the writer's age *twice told the period fpent on ftubborn Troy*, and you ftill leave him more than 40, when he fate down to the miferable fiege of *court* favour. He has before told us,

" A fool at forty is a fool indeed."

After all, the fiege feems to have been raifed only in confequence of what the General thought his *death-bed*.

Ib. l. ult. *add*, This enviable praife is due to Young. Can it be claimed by every writer?

P. 412. l. 21. *add*, Report has been accuftomed to call Altamont Lord Eufton.

P. 413. l. 7—15. *r*. The lively Letter in profe on *Original Compofition*, addreffed to Richardfon the author of *Clariffa*, appeared in 1759. Though he defpairs " of " breaking through the frozen obftructions of age " and care's incumbent cloud, into that flow of " thought and brightnefs of expreffion which fub- " jects fo polite require;" yet is it more like the production of untamed, unbridled youth, than of jaded fourfcore. Some fevenfold volumes put him in mind

mind of Ovid's sevenfold channels of the Nile at the conflagration;

———————————— ostia septem
Pulverulenta vocant, septem sine flumine valles.

Such leaden labours are like Lycurgus's iron money, which was so much less in value than in bulk, that it required barns for strong boxes and a yoke of oxen to draw five hundred pounds.

If there is a famine of invention in the land, we must travel, he says, like Joseph's brethren, far for food; we must visit the remote and rich antients. But an inventive genius may safely stay at home; that, like the widow's curse, is divinely replenished from within, and affords us a miraculous delight. He asks why it should seem altogether impossible, that Heaven's latest editions of the human mind may be the most correct and fair? And Jonson, he tells us, was very learned, as Sampson was very strong, to his own hurt. Blind to the nature of tragedy, he pulled down all antiquity on his head, and buried himself under it.

Is this " care's incumbent cloud," or " the frozen obstructions of age?"

In this letter Pope is severely censured for his " fall " from Homer's numbers, free as air, lofty and har- " monious as the spheres, into childish shackles and " tinkling sounds; for putting Achilles in petticoats " a second time;"—but we are told that the dying swan talked over an Epic plan with Young a few weeks before his decease.

Young's chief inducement to write this letter was, as he confesses, that he might erect a monumental marble to the memory of an old friend. He, who employed his pious pen for almost the last time in thus doing justice to the exemplary death-bed of Addison, might probably, at the close of his own life, afford no unuseful lesson for the deaths of others. In the postscript he writes to Richardson, that he will see in his next how far Addison is an original. But no other appears.

P. 416. l. 5. *add*, To Mrs. Montagu, the famous champion of Shakspeare, I am indebted for the history of *Resignation*. Observing that Mrs. Boscawen, in the midst of her grief for the loss of the admiral, derived consolation from the perusal of the *Night Thoughts*, Mrs. Montague proposed a visit to the author. From conversing with Young, Mrs. Boscawen derived still further consolation; and to that visit she and the world were indebted for this poem. It compliments Mrs. Montagu in the following lines:

> Yet, write I must. A Lady sues,
>   How shameful her request!
> My brain in labour with dull rhyme,
>   Her's teeming with the best!

And again —

> A friend you have, and I the same,
>   Whose prudent soft address
> Will bring to life those healing thoughts
>   Which died in your distress.
>
> That friend, the spirit of my theme
>   Extracting for your ease,
> Will leave to me the dreg, in thoughts
>   Too common; such as these.

By the same Lady I am enabled to say, in her own words, that Young's unbounded genius appeared to greater advantage

advantage in the companion, than even in the author—that the christian was in him a character still more inspired, more enraptured, more sublime than the poet—and that, in his ordinary conversation,

—letting down the golden chain from high,
He drew his audience upward to the sky.

Notwithstanding Young had said, in his *Conjecture on original Composition*, that " blank verse is verse unfallen, " uncurst; verse reclaimed, reinthroned in the true " language of the Gods"—notwithstanding he administred consolation to his own grief in this immortal language——Mrs. Boscawen was comforted in rhyme.

While the poet and the christian were applying this comfort, Young had himself occasion for comfort, in consequence of the sudden death of Richardson, who was printing the former part of the poem. Of Richardson's death he says——

When heaven would kindly set us free,
And earth's enchantment end;
It takes the most effectual means,
And robs us of a friend.

P. 418. l. 2. *add*, He had performed no duty for the last three or four years of his life, but he retained his intellects to the last.

Ib. *Instead of* l. 18—21. r. During some part of his life Young was abroad, but I have not been able to learn any particulars.

In his seventh Satire he says,

When, after battle, I the field have *seen*
Spread o'er with ghastly shapes which once were *men*.

And it is known that from this or from some other *field* he once wandered into the enemy's camp, with a claffic in his hand, which he was reading intently; and had some difficulty to prove that he was only an absent poet and not a spy.

P. 421. l. 8. *add*, Again Young was a poet; and again, with reverence be it spoken, poets by profeſſion do not make the beſt clergymen. If the Author of the *Night Thoughts* compoſed many ſermons, he did not oblige the public with many.

P. 424. l. 17. *add*, Is it not ſtrange that the Author of the *Night Thoughts* has inſcribed no monument to the memory of his lamented wife? Yet what marble will endure as long as the poems?

Ib. *at bottom, add*, P. S. This account of Young was ſeen by you in manuſcript you know, Sir; and, though I could not prevail on you to make any alterations, you inſiſted on ſtriking out one paſſage, only becauſe it ſaid, that, if I did not wiſh you to live long for your ſake, I did for the ſake of myſelf and of the world. But this poſtſcript you will not ſee before it is printed; and I will ſay here, in ſpite of you, how I feel myſelf honoured and bettered by your friendſhip—and that, if I do credit to the church, for which I am now going to give in exchange the bar, though not at ſo late a period of life as Young took Orders, it will be owing, in no ſmall meaſure, to my having had the happineſs of calling the Author of *The Rambler* my friend.   H. C.

Oxford, Sept. 1782.

P. 426. l. 16. *r.* and his points.

P. 428. l. 2. *r.* reſtrained by confinement to rhyme.

MAL-

ADDITIONS IN VOL. IV.

MALLET.

P. 442. l. 18. *add*, This he sold to Vaillant for one hundred and twenty pounds.

AKENSIDE.

P. 452. l. ult. *add*, Both are for a while equally exposed to laughter, but both are not therefore equally contemptible.

P. 457. l. 23. *r.* such self-indulgence.

P. 458. l. 4. *r.* His diction is certainly poetical as it is not prosaic, and elegant as it is not vulgar.

P. 459. l. 3. *add*, One great defect of his poem is very properly censured by Mr. *Walker*, unless it may be said in his defence, that what he has omitted was not properly in his plan. " His picture of man is grand
" and beautiful, but unfinished; the immortality of
" the soul, which is the natural consequence of the
" appetites and powers she is invested with, is
" scarcely once hinted throughout the poem. This
" deficiency is amply supplied by the masterly pencil
" of Dr. Young; who, like a good philosopher, has
" invincibly proved the immortality of man, from
" the grandeur of his conceptions, and the mean-
" ness and misery of his state; for this reason, a few
" passages are selected from the Night Thoughts,
" which, with those from Akenside, seem to form a
" complete view of the powers, situation and end of
" man." *Exercises for improvement in Elocution*, p. 66.

GRAY.

GRAY.

P. 463. l. 6. r. under the care of Mr. Antrobus, his mother's brother, then assistant to Dr. George.

P. 465. l. 13. r. or professing to like them.

P. 466. l. 11. r. It may be collected from the narrative.

P. 466. l. 22—25. r. which adds little to Gray's character.

P. 468. l. 12. add, and, it is said, by pranks yet more offensive and contemptuous.

P. 469. l. 2. r. the fashion to admire.

Ib. l. 19. r. Professor of Modern History.

P. 470. l. 18. r. The Professorship of History.

P. 471. l. 18. r. from a letter written to my friend Mr. Boswell, by the Reverend Mr. Temple, rector of St. Gluvias in Cornwall, and am as willing as his warmest well-wisher to believe it true.

LYTTELTON.

P. 490. l. 16. r. was commissioner of the Admiralty.

P. 491. l. 1. r. was at last hunted from his places.

Ib. l. 8. r. Mr. Lyttelton became his secretary.

Ib. l. 13. r. Mallet was made under-secretary with 200l. and Thomson had a pension of 100l. a year.

P. 494. l. 22. r. by much attention.

P. 495. l. 1. r. As he continued his activity.

P. 496. l. 8. r. without any conclusion.

Ib. l. 14. r. returned, in a note which I have read, acknowledgements which can never be proper, since they must be paid either for flattery or justice.

Ib. l. 20. r. losing with the rest his employment.

P. 498. l. 13. r. the style of Doctor. Something uncommon, &c.

Ib. l. 16. r. to the Doctor's edition is appended, &c.

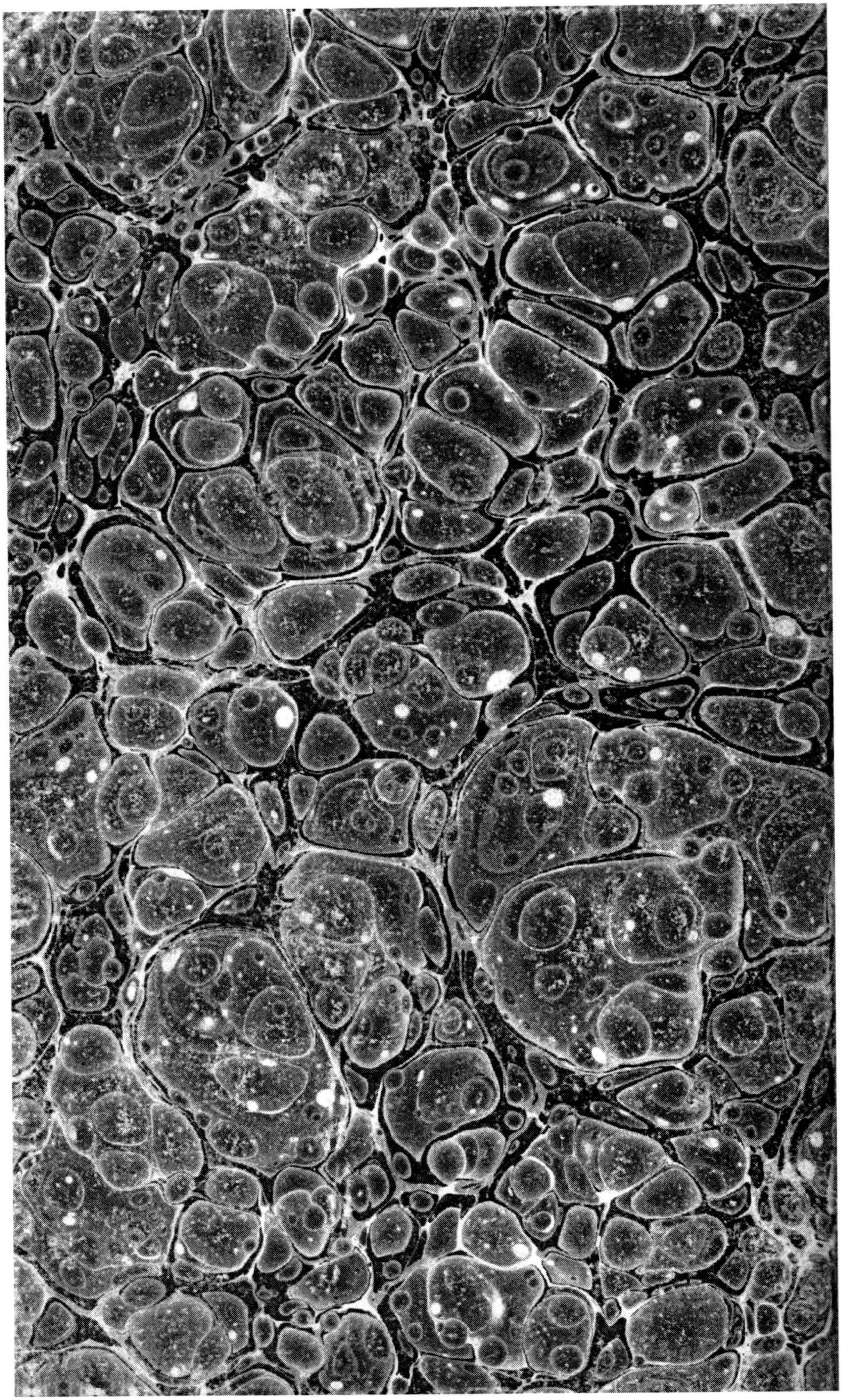

Lightning Source UK Ltd.
Milton Keynes UK
UKOW021931130213

206255UK00004B/114/P